Baptism Holy Ghost Prayer Book: How to Minister the Baptism of the Holy Ghost to Yourself and Others

PIUS JOSEPH © 2019 All Rights Reserved

The facts herein provided is truthful in all its entirety and coherent, in that no legal responsibility, in the form of consideration or else by the use or misuse of any teaching or directions contained within shall lie against.

The information offered here is for the purposes of spiritual upliftment and growth only. The author is aware that the application of this book may differ from one person to another as such things as faith, persistence, trust, and love for God can determine the outcomes that you receive from the application of the principles in this book.

Unless otherwise indicated, all scriptural quotations are taken from the King James Version © 1988-2007   Bible Soft Inc.

TABLE OF CONTENTS

DEDICATION   6

CHAPTER 1   1

WATERING THE GROUND FOR THE BAPTISM OF THE HOLY GHOST   2

CHAPTER 2   8

CONFESS THOSE SINS   8
CLEANSING BY THE BLOOD OF JESUS   10
RELEASING EVERY HURT   12
THE BITTER HEART   14

CHAPTER 3   18

DISTRACTION   19
PRAYER AGAINST DISTRACTION   21
SUSTAINING DESIRE   22
PRAYER   23
EXPECTATION   24
PRAYER FOR THE FULFILMENT OF GOD'S PROMISES   25
PRAYER   32

CHAPTER 4   35

THE MOMENT OF PRAYER	35
MINISTERING THE BAPTISM OF THE HOLY GHOST TO OTHERS	38
PRAYER FOR UTTERANCE	44

CHAPTER 5   48

| THE PRAYER THAT OPENS TONGUES | 48 |
| PRAYER OF THANKSGIVING FOR THE BAPTISM OF THE HOLY GHOST EVIDENCE BY TONGUE SPEAKING | 54 |

CHAPTER 6   58

| NEVER QUITTING | 58 |
| PRAYER TO WAIT AND BE FIRM | 64 |

CHAPTER 7   67

PRAYERS AFTER BAPTISM	67
PRAYER FOR CLARITY OF HIS VOICE	69
PRAYER	71
PRAYER FOR OBEDIENCE	72
GRIEVING THE HOLY SPIRIT	74
PRAYER	79
PRAYER FOR THE USE OF SPIRITUAL GIFTS	79

CHAPTER 8   90

| YOUR FAITH AND BAPTISM | 90 |
| PRAYER | 94 |

THE RIVERS OF LIVING WATER	94
PRAYER	96
FREE E-BOOK FOR YOU!!!	98
OTHER BOOKS BY THE SAME AUTHOR	99

DEDICATION

This Book is dedicated to God Almighty who gave me the inspiration to write this book. I also dedicate this book to all those who desired to be filled with the Holy Ghost evidenced by praying in tongues, and those who want to pray for another to receive the baptism of the Holy Ghost.

Acts 2:39-40

For the promise is unto you, and to your children, and to all that are afar off, even as many as the Lord our God shall call.

CHAPTER 1

After the release of the Baptism of the Holy Ghost: Easy Ways to Be Filled with the Holy Spirit and Obtain the Gift of the Spirit. It became apparent that there need to be a prayer book or a handbook that will help the believer to pray for himself in order to receive the baptism of the Holy Ghost with the evidence of speaking in tongues.

I was in the car going to work when this inspiration stung my mind. I decided to work on this book right away. It was this singular encounter on that day that gave birth to this book that you are now holding in your hands.

Watering the Ground for the Baptism of the Holy Ghost

To me, the actual process of preparing someone to receive the baptism of the Holy Spirit in his life is important as the baptism of the spirit itself. If some things aren't done away with, they may hinder the baptism of the Holy Spirit in the life of that person. That is why I place a high value on preparing a believer to receive the baptism of the Holy Spirit. And I believe that my perspective is not wrong. What is the whole purpose of salvation? Is it not for God to put his spirit upon you so that you can live a life that will give glory to his name? First, let us look at it. God calls you out of darkness and you heard his call (1 Peter 2:9). You gladly answer the call and shouting glory to God because you are saved. God then pours a measure of the spirit upon your life. Then you come to realize that there be a Holy

Ghost (Acts 19:2). You prayed for the baptism of the Holy Spirit and you are filled. Then, you grew up in the spirit and made use of your gift to change the world around you. Many became saved through your life or your calling as a child of God. What started as a plan of salvation led to the baptism of the Holy Spirit and to a successful Christian life. I do not want to go further, but the importance of preparing a believer for the baptism of the Holy Spirit with the evidence of speaking in tongues cannot be overemphasized.

I know that this book is a prayer book and all that you expect from it are series of prayer. However, there are certain explanations that without them, this prayer book on the baptism of the Holy Ghost won't be complete. Before you rush into prayer, wait and listen to what I have to say. This is necessary so that you don't go and pray and you don't see results from your prayer for the baptism of the Holy Ghost with the evidence of speaking in tongues. I presume that you have already read the book on the baptism of the Holy Ghost, but if you haven't you can get it from here.

Before the baptism of the Holy Ghost comes upon you, it is essential that the ground is watered. For a plant to grow, certain atmospheric conditions must be met. This includes the fact that the soil must be in the right condition, the sun and other conditions which must be present before germination can take place.

This same principle applies to the baptism of the Holy Ghost as well. I want you to use this prayer book and get results. I equally want you to pray on your own and be baptized. Therefore, you must be spiritually prepared before you begin the prayers in this book.

Once you are prepared, you will find it very easy to minister the baptism of the Holy Ghost on yourself. You won't need a pastor to pray over you. Neither will you need a believer to lay his hand on you. By simply following the principles of prayer outlined in this book, you will be able to get filled in the Holy Ghost with the evidence of speaking in tongues. If you want to know what will happen to you after the baptism of the Holy Ghost, you can get this free e-book of mine that contains all the information that you need on that subject.

This is a handbook on prayer for the baptism of the Holy Ghost with the evidence of speaking in tongues. It can be used anywhere. You can use these principles outlined in this book and minister the baptism of the Holy Ghost on anyone, and the person by the grace of God will be filled. The principles of God are without limitation. It has no respect for territorial jurisdiction or for a race. Whenever the word of God is rightly applied, results are apparent.

Using the guide explained in this book, I have prayed over several people, and I have seen them filled. I have prayed over kids, and I have seen them baptized with the Holy Ghost and spoke in tongues. By the mercies of God, I have prayed for people over the phone from different parts of the world and they were filled with the Holy Ghost. This has made me understand that the principles of the word of God are without limitation. The key thing is to apply the principles rightly, once done in that manner, the person must be filled because God has promised that he would do that.

Hebrews 10:19

*Having therefore,
brethren, boldness to
enter into the holiest by
the blood of Jesus,*

CHAPTER 2

Confess Those Sins

Unconfessed and unrepented sin will not only stop you from receiving the baptism of the Holy Ghost, but it will also hinder you from making heaven itself.

1 John 1:9

> *If we confess our sins, he is faithful and just to forgive us our sins, and to cleanse us from all unrighteousness.*

1 John 2:1-2

1 My little children, these things write I unto you, that ye sin not. And if any man sin, we have an advocate with the Father, Jesus Christ the righteous:

2 And he is the propitiation for our sins: and not for ours only, but also for the sins of the whole world.

Hebrews 4: 15-17

15 For we have not an high priest which cannot be touched with the feeling of our infirmities; but was in all points tempted like as we are, yet without sin.

16 Let us therefore come boldly unto the throne of grace, that we may obtain mercy, and find grace to help in time of need.

Father in the mighty name of Jesus, I come before you today to ask you for mercy over all of my sins. I ask that you cleanse my heart from secret and open faults in the name of Jesus, Amen. Wash me from every sin that may be in my heart the ones I know and the ones I'm not aware of, sins of commission and omission in the name of Jesus, Amen.

Cleansing by the Blood of Jesus

Hebrews 9:12-14

12 Neither by the blood of goats and calves, but by his own blood he entered in once into the holy place, having obtained eternal redemption for us.

13 For if the blood of bulls and of goats, and the ashes of an heifer sprinkling the unclean, sanctifieth to the purifying of the flesh:

14 How much more shall the blood of Christ, who through the eternal Spirit offered himself without spot to God, purge your conscience from dead works to serve the living God?

1 John 1:7

But if we walk in the light, as he is in the light, we have fellowship one with another, and the blood of Jesus Christ his Son cleanseth us from all sin.

Hebrews 10:19

Having therefore, brethren, boldness to enter into the holiest by the blood of Jesus,

Father in the mighty name of Jesus I make demands on the blood of Jesus Christ your Son to cleanse me from all of my sins this very moment in the name of Jesus. I ask that the blood of Jesus will wash my heart, my soul, and my spirit in the name of Jesus. For I know that the blood of your Son has the capacity to cleanse me from all of my fault and sin so that I can receive the baptism of the Holy Ghost as promised afore in the Bible. In Jesus name, I pray, Amen.

Releasing Every Hurt

Perhaps the first place to begin our prayer is at this point. Unforgiveness is one of the greatest hindrances to receiving the baptism of the Holy Ghost evidenced by speaking in tongues. Throughout the whole Bible, God has consistently been asking us to forgive those who hurt us. A heart check is, therefore, necessary before you begin to pray for the baptism of the Holy Ghost. This principle of forgiveness is so fundamentally important that the Bible tells us that if we have a gift to offer to the Lord and we remember that someone has offended us, we are to drop it right at the altar go back and settled that hurt.

Matthew 5:23-24

Therefore if thou bring thy gift to the altar, and there rememberest that thy brother hath ought against thee;

24 Leave there thy gift before the altar, and go thy way; first be reconciled to thy brother, and then come and offer thy gift.

Father in the mighty name of Jesus, I pray that you bring to my remembrance everyone who has hurt me that I may forgive them in Jesus name. I release from my heart everybody that offended me today in the name of Jesus. I pray that you forgive them all because it is possible that they do not even know that they offended me in the name of Jesus, Amen. And as I have forgiven them, I also receive forgiveness for my sins for violating your word because you told me to forgive all who have hurt me, in Jesus name.

The Bitter Heart

Offenses will come! Let us be very clear about that. For as long as you live in a world occupied by people, you will be angered, offended and wronged. But do not hold them in your heart. Bitterness comes when someone has offended you and you hold it up in your heart. Bitterness and unforgiveness are twins. The Bible says in Hebrews 12:15 that bitterness defiles. And if you are defiled, you can't be filled. There are so many people who are crying to God to be filled with his Spirit, yet they are bitter against someone. They are holding grudges against the person who has wronged or offended them. You have to clear your heart from these things before the Lord can fill you with his Holy Spirit.

People will offend you and get you angry. But know that once you hold onto the offense in your heart, it becomes bitterness. Bitterness defiles the heart so much. When a man is bitter, his heart is

Baptism of the Holy Ghost Prayer Book

defiled and this makes it impossible for the Holy Spirit to come and dwell in him (Hebrews 12:15). The Bible says once the root of bitterness develops in your heart, it will defile you. The Holy Ghost cannot occupy a defiled vessel.

When people offend you or have wronged you, release them from your heart. Never hold that against them. Don't allow the thought to linger in your heart. Sometimes, when you are offended, it is easy to allow the offenders to rent a space in your heart. The thought of what to do in return will occupy your heart. If you keep thinking of the offense, the root of bitterness is gradually growing, and it will defile you. This will hinder you from receiving the baptism of the Holy Ghost.

Hebrews 12:15

Looking diligently lest any man fail of the grace of God; lest any root of bitterness springing up trouble you, and thereby many be defiled;

Matthew 15:13

But he answered and said, Every plant, which my heavenly Father hath not planted, shall be rooted up.

Father in the mighty name of Jesus, I make demands on your grace and your help to remove every root of bitterness in my heart. You said in your word that everything that you have not planted in my life as your child will be removed from its roots. Therefore, I ask you today that you pull down every stronghold of bitterness in my heart that may serve as a hindrance to receiving the baptism of the Holy Ghost. I ask this in the mighty name of Jesus.

Proverbs 23:18

*For surely there is an end;
and thine expectation
shall not be cut off.*

Chapter 3

The baptism of the Holy Ghost is an essential encounter that every believer must have. It is true that the baptism of the Holy Ghost can minister through the laying on of hands, yet you can minister the Holy Ghost baptism by yourself without anyone praying for you. That is the essence of this book to give you a practical guide for praying the baptism of the Holy Ghost into your life or into the life of another person.

The prayers that you have prayed so far, are preliminary prayers. They are meant to prepare you for the actual ministration of the baptism of the Holy Ghost. By the grace and mercies of God, I have applied some of these prayer principles with great results.

Distraction

Before ministering the baptism of the Holy Ghost remove all forms of distraction from your immediate environment. This becomes necessary when the distractions are physical and can be curtailed by taking practical actions. Granted that certain distractions can be physically handled, like the TV playing, the distraction from the radio, noise and so many other things that can hinder from you concentrating in order to receive the baptism of the Holy Ghost, yet when distractions are spiritual how do you handle them? If it is a phone, you can put it off to avoid incoming calls from constituting a distraction, preventing you from getting filled.

Spiritual distraction must, however, be handled differently. When Jesus gave instruction to his disciples to wait on the promise of the Father, the disciples didn't go to the grocery store or to a sports stadium and say "brethren let us tarry here and wait." But they went to the upper room, and the reason for their choice of environment is not far fetched from the need to eliminate all forms of distraction that may stop them from receiving the promise of the father.

This must not be confused with the Holy Ghost coming upon you while you are driving or in an environment that you never expected. I had a sister in one of our online classes who had got in filled without knowing. She had joined the class believing God to be filled in the Holy Ghost with the evidence of speaking in tongues. Unknown to her that had already happened. The Bible says my people perish for lack of knowledge. I prayed for her and immediately she began to speak in tongues. I later realized

Baptism of the Holy Ghost Prayer Book

that she was already filled with the Holy Ghost but, she didn't know. That sister had her encounter in a different environment even though it was not a quiet one. Those are some of the rare cases where the Holy Ghost can come upon you even when you are in a public environment. However, in most cases, it is advisable to do away with every distraction.

Prayer against Distraction

1 Corinthians 7:35

> *And this I speak for your own profit; not that I may cast a snare upon you, but for that which is comely, and that ye may attend upon the Lord without distraction.*

Father in the name of Jesus, I pray that every form of distraction that may stand as a hindrance to the baptism of the Holy Ghost be removed right now in the name of Jesus. I ask that you help my heart to be totally focused on you while I believe and trust you to fill me with the Holy Ghost, in the name of Jesus. I take authority over every spirit of distraction as I pray for the baptism of the Holy Ghost, in Jesus name Amen.

In the mighty name of Jesus, I pray that you keep my mind stayed on you even as I pray right at this hour in Jesus name. I pray against the wondering mind, distractions, and inability to keep my mind stayed on you in the place of prayer in Jesus name.

Sustaining Desire

The Bible says blessed are those who hunger and thirst after righteousness for they shall be satisfied. It is a righteous thing to desire the baptism of the Holy Ghost. Since the baptism of the Holy Ghost is a righteous thing, the Bible says those who desire it will surely be filled.

Prayer

Isaiah 65:24

And it shall come to pass, that before they call, I will answer; and while they are yet speaking, I will hear.

Father in the name of Jesus, I pray that you fill me with the hunger and passion to be filled with your spirit in the name of Jesus. I ask that you pour into my life the passion and hunger to be baptized, in Jesus name Amen. I believe in your word that whenever we hunger and thirst after righteous things, you will always bring that hunger and thirst to a complete state of satisfaction in Jesus name, Amen. The grace to desire the baptism of the spirit is released upon me now in the name of Jesus. Thank you, Lord, in Jesus name, Amen.

Your desire has the capacity to magnetize spiritual things in your direction. If your desire is to be filled with the Holy Spirit as you pray, God knows that. God answers the thoughts of your mind just the way he answers your prayers. Before you even open your mouth, God will answer.

Expectation

Proverbs 23:18

> *For surely there is an end; and thine expectation shall not be cut off.*

Father in the name of Jesus, I pray that you give me an expectant heart as I pray for the baptism of the Holy Ghost with the evidence of speaking in tongues, in Jesus name, Amen. My trust is fully in your word that the expectation of every righteous man shall never fail, in Jesus mighty name we pray, Amen.

Father in the name of Jesus, I have come to restate what you said in your word that my desire will be met according to your word in Jesus name. I come to you today with a heart full of expectation that my baptism in the Holy Ghost will take place at this moment in Jesus name, Amen.

Prayer for the Fulfilment of God's Promises

The baptism of the Holy Ghost is a gift as well as a promise. You need to have this understanding from the beginning as it will help you to receive the Holy Ghost into your life. There are numerous scriptures in the Bible that explain that the baptism of the Holy Ghost is a gift. A believer who is asking God for the infilling of the Holy Ghost for himself or another must come from this perspective. Towards this end, you are to gather Scriptures that speak about the coming of the Holy Ghost as the fulfillment of that promise. For instance, Scriptures such as Luke 11:13, John 16:13, John 14:26, John 15:26, John 14:17, and Acts 1:8.

When praying the baptism of the Holy Ghost, let your prayers be garnished with these Scriptures. Scripture-based prayers are the greatest way to pray the baptism of the Holy Ghost into the lives of believers.

If the person you are praying for to receive the baptism of the Holy Ghost does not know anything about the spirit of God, it is important to acquaint him with the knowledge of the Holy Ghost before you start praying the baptism of the Holy Ghost into his life. Please, do not get me wrong. It is possible for someone who has never heard anything about the Holy Ghost to be baptized immediately. Subsequently, blast in tongues like never before. That is the dimension of the power of God – he is limitless.

However, in most instances, it is better to prepare the person before you pray the baptism of the Holy Ghost upon his life. In that way, the child of God is placed in the better position to receive the Holy Ghost into his life and to begin to enjoy the fruit of the promise of God that says ye shall receive power after the Holy Ghost has come upon you, and ye shall be my witnesses in Judaea, Jerusalem, and uttermost part of the earth. The question somebody may be attempting to ask is, brother Pius, is that in the scripture. Yes, it is. Let us look at it.

Acts 19:2-3

> *He said unto them, Have ye received the Holy Ghost since ye believed? And they said unto him, We have not so much as heard whether there be any Holy Ghost.*

When the people in the above Scripture said that they didn't even know who the Holy Ghost is, Paul the apostle had to give them a brief explanation of who the Holy Ghost is.

Acts 19:3-4

3 And he said unto them, Unto what then were ye baptized? And they said, Unto John's baptism.

4 Then said Paul, John verily baptized with the baptism of repentance, saying unto the people, that they should believe on him which should come after him, that is, on Christ Jesus.

There are many people around the world who know nothing about the Holy Spirit. Remember what the Bible says that he is the spirit that the world cannot receive. They do not know him. Some people who have been going to church as normal Christians, even they too, may need a small explanation of who the Holy Spirit is. I believe personally that, whenever someone is prepared to receive the baptism of the Holy Ghost the ministration of the spirit of God becomes easier. I have seen this manifested in the lives of so many people around the world.

After going through the online baptism class, the prayer doesn't literally take a long time before they are filled with the Holy Ghost evidenced by speaking in tongues.

If the Apostle Paul practiced it, then it is something that we need to imbibe in order to pray for others to receive the baptism of the Holy Ghost or when we are ministering the baptism of the Holy Ghost upon our lives. A person who is undertaking a self-ministration of the baptism of the Holy Spirit, all he needs to do after reading the Bible and some materials on the subject of the Holy Spirit is to pray for the baptism of the Holy Ghost; he will receive it.

Acts 19:5

When they heard this, they were baptized in the name of the Lord Jesus.

After Paul told them a little about the Holy Spirit and that John the Baptist only baptized with water unto repentance. And that they should look unto him who will baptize them with the Holy Ghost and with fire. Immediately the people heard this brief explanation of the Holy Spirit, they were amazed. Paul the apostle was able to arouse the hunger of the people about the baptism of the Holy Ghost. I can tell you that, whenever a man is hungry for the baptism of the Holy Spirit, it doesn't take long before the person is filled with the Holy Ghost and speaking in tongues.

After Paul had his brief explanation about the Holy Spirit, the people were already prepared. The hunger for the baptism of the Holy Spirit had reached the summit.

Look at what happened after Paul had prepared the mind of the people to receive the baptism of the Holy Spirit with the evidence of speaking in tongues.

Acts 19:6

And when Paul had laid his hands upon them, the Holy Ghost came on them; and they spake with tongues, and prophesied.

The moment the hand of Paul touched their foreheads, the Holy Spirit came upon the people. They began to pray in tongues instantly. What astounded me is that they not only spoke in tongues, the gift of prophecy was immediately activated in their lives. Hallelujah! The preparation that Paul did had spark hunger in the hearts of these people. And because they were so hungry, they were able to magnetize other gifts of the spirit that accompany the baptism of the Holy Spirit. There was a time I was praying for a sister in Texas, Corpus Christi, to receive the baptism of the Holy Spirit. After our Facebook class online, the sister was desperately hungry for the baptism of the Holy Spirit to come upon her life. I called her without notice and asked her if she was ready to receive the baptism of the Holy Spirit with the evidence of speaking in tongues. At first, she was hesitant. But later she agreed. It wasn't long before she started speaking in tongues after I had prayed for her. She also sang in tongues too. I believe that the hungrier a believer is to receive the baptism of the Holy Spirit, the easier it is for the power to come upon him. And this is in line with Scriptures that says that blessed are those who hunger and thirst after righteousness for they shall be satisfied.

Prayer

Thank you Lord, because of your promises in the book of (insert Scriptures about the promises of the Holy Spirit, e.g., John 16:13, John 14:26, Acts 1:8, et cetera) that you have made the promise to fill me with the baptism of the Holy Spirit with the evidence of speaking in tongues. Lord, I thank you because today, these Scriptures will be fulfilled in my life. Let your name be praised because of

Baptism of the Holy Ghost Prayer Book

this promise and to you be all the glory, in Jesus name Amen.

Father, I thank you, because of the reality of your promise today. Thank you for this dear brother/sister... (Mention the name of the person you are praying for to receive the baptism of the Holy Spirit if you can). I believe today is my day for the baptism of the Holy Ghost to be made manifest in my life. Thank you, father, because the Holy Spirit will fill me to overflow today. In the name of Jesus, Amen.

Acts

But ye shall receive power, after that the Holy Ghost is come upon you: and ye shall be witnesses unto me both in Jerusalem, and in all Judaea, and in Samaria, and unto the uttermost part of the earth.

CHAPTER 4

The Moment of Prayer

The ministration of the baptism of the Holy Ghost in the life of a believer is an important moment for the infilling of the spirit. It is at this moment that the highest level of focus and concentration is required. Every form of distraction must be shutout at this point. If that is not done, it is possible to miss out on the baptism of the Holy Spirit with the evidence of speaking in tongues. If you are ministering the baptism of the Holy Ghost on yourself, it is important to constantly check your spirit man.

Oftentimes, God will baptize you, and a strange language will begin to form in your heart. This is in line with what Jesus preached when he said that those who believe in me out of their belly shall flow fountains of living water.

John 7:38

> *He that believeth on me, as the scripture hath said, out of his belly shall flow rivers of living water.*

When this new language begins to boil deep in your spirit man, it is important to give it expression. Some believers who are experiencing the baptism of the Holy Ghost for the first time in their lives often encountered this problem. While some of them may be complaining that the Holy Spirit has not yet been poured on them, a critical examination will show that the Holy Ghost has already come upon them with the evidence of speaking in tongues. This small language they hear deep

Baptism of the Holy Ghost Prayer Book

within their spirit was stifled and never given expression. It is, therefore, necessary to constantly check your spirit to know if the language of the spirit is beginning to crystallize in your heart. This is where many believers missed it. God will always pour his spirit upon you so that you can speak in tongues, but it is your responsibility to give expression to the language of the spirit in your heart. Even if you don't feel it in your heart, your tongue can become heavy with spiritual language trying to gain expression through your mouth. When this happens, open your mouth and speak. The Bible says something important in the book of Psalms 81:10:

I am the Lord thy God, which brought thee out of the land of Egypt: open thy mouth wide, and I will fill it.

Here the Bible is saying that if you can open your mouth God will fill it with tongues. The problem is many believers are not willing to open their mouths when they begin to experience the language of the spirit in their hearts.

Ministering the baptism of the Holy Ghost to Others

If you are ministering the baptism of the Holy Ghost with evidence of speaking in tongues on others, it is important to note this critical factor. If it is the will of God to baptize them once you begin to pray, then glory to God for that. However, God is a dynamic father and he may choose to operate in different ways with the same prayer request. If he doesn't pour his spirit upon them at an instant, you need to guide them so that they can give expression to what they are hearing in their spirit man. When you have prayed for a while and found that they are struggling, pause and ask them if they hear any language in their hearts. If the answer to your inquiry is in the affirmative, that they are hearing strange language in their heart, then tell them to speak what they are hearing. Even the disciples had to speak in tongues before the Holy Ghost gave them utterance.

Acts 2: 4

And they were all filled with the Holy Ghost, and began to speak with other tongues, as the Spirit gave them utterance.

The translation of the word utterance from the original Greek means **apophtheggomai** which is translated to mean speak forth or pronounced. Speaking in tongues is a language of the spirit, and it is only the Holy Spirit that has the power to give you the ability to pronounce each of the linguistic sentences you hear in your spirit man. That's what is called utterance, the spirit empowering you to pray as you should. When people are struggling to utter the language of the spirit which is rumbling in their mouths, you can ask God to give them utterance.

Recently, I was praying for my friend's fiancé to be baptized in the Holy Spirit. I had prayed for a long time and nothing happened. But when I enquired of the spirit of God, I felt within me that she had been baptized. While this may not be physically true, it is true in the realm of the spirit. A brother that I know came and asked her to speak what she was hearing in her heart. As she obeyed the direction of this brother in Christ, she began to speak in tongues in a few minutes.

When you begin to give expression to the things that you are hearing in your spirit, the Holy Spirit takes that act of faith from you and give you the ability to be able to speak clearly that which you hear. It is possible to hear a single sentence of tongues in your spirit man. Yet you need to speak what you are hearing. And as you do so, the Holy Spirit will enable you to speak more and more.

As someone who is ministering the baptism of the Holy Ghost to another person, you need to check some of the things we have discussed here. Many people aren't aware of these things so they will just say, "oh, he never came upon me. Even though I prayed very well. And several people also laid their hands on me." When you scrutinize this kind of statement, you will notice that the person had already been baptized but the failure to give expression to what the spirit has already done was the chief problem. If only they could open their mouths, God will fill it with tongues of fire.

If you look at the book of Acts 2:1- 5, you will see that one of the operative words of the Scripture, ***they were all filled with the Holy Ghost.*** " This is in line with what Jesus had told them in the book of Luke 11:13

If ye then, being evil, know how to give good gifts unto your children: how much more shall your heavenly Father give the Holy Spirit to them that ask him?

In further confirmation of these Scriptures, the Bible says in the book of Acts 2:39:

For the promise is unto you, and to your children, and to all that are afar off, even as many as the Lord our God shall call.

The Scripture confirms that it is God's desire to baptize every believer with the Holy Spirit. I know that this is a prayer book and all that it should contain ought to be prayers. But this explanation of scriptural truth is necessary for your understanding and effective ministration of the baptism of the Holy Ghost on yourself and any other person you may be praying for. If the Scripture says the baptism of the Holy Ghost or the gift of the Holy Ghost is for you and all of your children, then anybody with any assertion that says that speaking in tongues is a gift and that everyone must not speak in tongues is saying that in error. The statement may only be true to the extent that it is the gift of the spirit of God and no more. The Bible even says that we should earnestly desire the gift of the spirit. And from the Scriptures we have seen so far, anyone can be baptized with the Holy Ghost evidenced by tongue-speaking. I have seen adults and kids baptized with the Holy Ghost and they spoke in tongues. This understanding is necessary for the believer in our day.

You must also note that it is possible for the tongue to be loosed to speak clearly. This is necessary when the person has already been baptized but is struggling to speak the words in his mouth. In situations like this, what you need to do is to pray to God to lose the tongue so that the person can speak as he ought to. If the person you are ministering to is actually struggling with the utterance, the tongues coming out from the mouth may not be clear and decipherable. If you are ministering the baptism of the Holy Ghost to someone, you lose the tongue for a clear language of the spirit to flow from it. If you are praying for yourself to receive the baptism of the spirit with the evidence of praying in tongues and you noticed that you have received the baptism of the spirit, but you are struggling to speak in tongues you ask God to lose your tongue so that you can pray fluently in the spirit.

Prayer for Utterance

Acts 2: 4

> *And they were all filled with the Holy Ghost, and began to speak with other tongues, as the Spirit gave them utterance.*

Father in the mighty name of Jesus, I pray for the empowerment of the spirit to be able to speak as I should in the name of Jesus. As I open my mouth to speak in tongues, I pray that you fill them to overflow so that I can pray in this new language of the spirit, in the name of Jesus. Amen.

Father in the name of Jesus, it is my prayer at this moment that you give me utterance to speak in tongues in the name of Jesus. As the Holy Spirit pours this new language on me, give me the grace to pronounce what I hear in my spirit man in the name of Jesus.

Father in the mighty name of Jesus, I make demands on the power of the Holy Spirit that can empower me to speak in tongues to be poured on me right now in Jesus name. I make demands on your help that it should be released on me right now to pray in tongues in the name of Jesus. For you say in your word, that the Holy Spirit will give us utterance to speak in tongues. I, therefore, ask for your help in the name of Jesus. Amen.

1 John 5:14-16

And this is the confidence that we have in him, that, if we ask any thing according to his will, he heareth us:

15 And if we know that he hear us, whatsoever we ask, we know that we have the petitions that we desired of him.

CHAPTER 5

The Prayer that Opens Tongues

One of the quickest ways to be baptized in the Holy Ghost with evidence of speaking in tongues is, to begin with, thanksgiving and appreciation to God. One of the obvious reasons why Jesus had tremendous results in his prayers while he was on earth is because he took very seriously the importance of appreciation and thanksgiving to God. This accounts for the reason why he found it very strange when he prayed for ten lepers and only one returned to give thanks to God.

Luke 17:14-19

14 And when he saw them, he said unto them, Go shew yourselves unto the priests. And it came to pass, that, as they went, they were cleansed.

15 And one of them, when he saw that he was healed, turned back, and with a loud voice glorified God,

16 And fell down on his face at his feet, giving him thanks: and he was a Samaritan.

17 And Jesus answering said, Were there not ten cleansed? but where are the nine?

18 There are not found that returned to give glory to God, save this stranger.

19 And he said unto him, Arise, go thy way: thy faith hath made thee whole.

This scripture captures what happens every time we give praise and thanksgiving to God for what he has done. While the nine of them were never thankful to God for what he has done for them, one of them returned back from the priest to give to God glory and thanks to Jesus for what he has done for him. It was only then that his miracle was perfected. This underscores the importance of thanksgiving. If you want to be baptized in the Holy Ghost with evidence of speaking in tongues, this is the first thing you must do when praying for the baptism of the Holy Ghost or ministering it to another person.

Before Jesus ever said a word concerning Lazarus, the first thing he did was Thanksgiving. After he has fully thanked his father, he prayed to God for the resurrection of his friend, Lazarus.

John 11:41

Then they took away the stone from the place where the dead was laid. And Jesus lifted up his eyes, and said, Father, I thank thee that thou hast heard me.

Having thanked his father, he knew that the miracle of resurrection was sure. He prayed; Lazarus was raised from the dead.

You need to imbibe this if what you want is the baptism of the Holy Ghost. Before you begin to minister the baptism of the Holy Ghost, start by thanking God for the baptism of the Holy Ghost itself. This is an act of faith. The Bible says without faith no man can please God for he that comes to God must believe first.

Hebrews 11:6

But without faith it is impossible to please him: for he that cometh to God must believe that he is, and that he

is a rewarder of them that diligently seek him.

Thanking God for what you are to receive before seeing it is considered as an act of faith. The Bible says faith is the substance of things hoped for, and the evidence of things not seen. By it, we understand that the elders obtained a good report. I think we need to look at that scripture very well. The Bible says by it the elders obtained a good report. In your own case, what is that report? I will say, the baptism of the Holy Spirit with evidence of speaking in tongues that you are expecting God to fulfill based on this promise of Scripture. The report can be a testimony. And that testimony is to the effect that, "I have been baptized with the Holy Spirit, and I can now speak in tongues."

So if you want to obtain a good report to the effect that you have been baptized in the Holy Spirit with the evidence of speaking in tongues, start by praising and thanking God.

If Jesus had to practice this, we are no exception. Each time we appreciate God for what he has not yet done, we are banking on his ability. And as we do that, he proves himself faithful by making true his promises. What is that promise? For your own case, we have to look at Scripture.

It is not far-fetched from the book of Acts 1:8 where the Bible captures it as follows:

But ye shall receive power, after that the Holy Ghost is come upon you: and ye shall be witnesses unto me both in Jerusalem, and in all Judaea, and in Samaria, and unto the uttermost part of the earth.

John 6:11

And Jesus took the loaves; and when he had given

thanks, he distributed to the disciples, and the disciples to them that were set down; and likewise of the fishes as much as they would.

When it was time for Jesus to pray on the bread, the first thing he did was to thank his father. Shortly after Thanksgiving, there was multiplication of the bread. The Bible record that many were fed excluding women and children.

Prayer of Thanksgiving for the Baptism of the Holy Ghost Evidence by Tongue Speaking

Father in the name of Jesus, I thank you for the fulfillment of the promise of the baptism of the Holy Ghost in my life today. I appreciate you because the promise has been made a reality in my life. I give you all the glory and all the honor because you have said in your word that the promise of the Holy Ghost is for me and for my children.

Baptism of the Holy Ghost Prayer Book

Father in the mighty name of Jesus, thank you for the utterance you have given unto me to speak in tongues today. Thank you for deciding to pour your spirit upon my life. Now, Jesus, I can speak in tongues.

Father in the mighty name of Jesus, I thank you for the power of the spirit that now works in my life. Thank you, father, because that power of the spirit has now given me the grace to speak in tongues, the language of the spirit that you have graciously given unto me. Thank you, my father, and to you be all the glory in the name of Jesus.

In Jesus name, I thank you for the cloven tongues of fire that now sits on my head. To you be all the glory in the name of Jesus. I trust in the power of the spirit that after this encounter with the power that created the earth, I will be truly changed in the name of Jesus. Thank you mighty father to you be all the glory, the honor, and the adoration in the name of Jesus, Amen.

Father in the name of Jesus, here I am to appreciate you for the fulfillment of the promise for the person I am praying for today. I know Lord Jesus that as you have promised you will also fulfill by releasing the Holy Spirit upon the life of this person in the mighty name of Jesus. I know that by the promise of your word that ye shall receive power after the Holy Ghost has come upon you I stand today upon that word unshaken that the baptism of the Holy Spirit evidenced by speaking in tongues will manifest in the life of this person in the name of Jesus.

Father in the name of Jesus I want to thank you for the ability and the grace of utterance that you have given to this one person that I am praying for today in the name of Jesus. I appreciate you dear father, in Jesus name. Amen.

1 Corinthians 16:13-14

Watch ye, stand fast in the faith, quit you like men, be strong.

Chapter 6

Never Quitting

God is faithful because his promises are ye and Amen. Whenever God has made his promise, what makes him God is that he has the ability to bring the promise to pass. And this also applies to you, who is currently reading this book at the moment.

The baptism of the Holy Ghost is of great importance to any believer so strive to get it. Never be discouraged! Now my belief is this. If you've prayed for the baptism of the Holy Ghost with the evidence of

Baptism of the Holy Ghost Prayer Book

speaking in tongues once, God is going to fill you with his spirit. Sometimes the baptism may not be instant. And that is what makes him God. He is dynamic, he is unique, and he does things at his own will.

By the mercies of God, I have prayed for several people and have seen them baptized with the Holy Ghost evidenced by tongue speaking. In the same vein, I have also prayed for people sometimes and they weren't filled. There is no possible explanation that can be proffered for situations like this. My obligation is to teach the word of God in truth and allow the people to apply the same principle for the baptism of the Holy Ghost with the evidence of praying in tongues. When I do that, God is always faithful to honor his word.

Sometimes these things happen. Your obligation as a minister is to check and see if the person is been hindered from been baptized as a result of a factor. After carrying out a check, you discovered that there is no inhibiting factor that is stopping the Holy Spirit from coming upon the life of the believer, what you need to do is to encourage the person to keep standing and trusting God to be filled with the Holy Ghost evidenced by speaking in tongues. Don't just give up and say, "I have prayed, God did not fill this person with his Holy Spirit."

No one can direct God on how to carry out the baptism of the Holy Ghost in the life of his children. He pours his spirit on the life of the believer by his will. However, it is worthy to note that, when the disciples gathered together to pray for the baptism of the Holy Spirit, they were all filled with the Holy Ghost (Acts 2:1-4).

The import of the scripture above is God has already committed himself to baptize all of his children if only they can ask him to do so and never give up because they didn't experience it at the time they prayed (Luke 11:13).

So, if you are praying for anybody to be filled with the Holy Ghost and it didn't happen immediately as you thought it should, don't give up easily. If you are praying for yourself to be filled with the baptism of the Holy Ghost; it didn't happen immediately, don't give up. Continue to stand in faith and believe God to fill you with the Holy Ghost.

When I started seeking the face of the Lord concerning the baptism of the Holy Ghost with the evidence of speaking in tongues, mine did not happen instantly. It took a while before I got filled. One day, I was in the midst of some brethren praying when a fervent brother saw me praying in English while others were praying in tongues. As soon as the brother noticed that, he came and met me and prayed for me. The prayer was powerful, yet I was not filled with the Holy Ghost. He then set a personal time of prayer with me to continue the ministration which he has started. All his determined effort were not successful. God had a different plan to fill me with the Holy Ghost.

I prayed for long seeking the face of the Lord for this particular encounter with the spirit of God. After waiting for about four months, I was praying one day on my own when suddenly a powerful force dragged my knees to the ground. Clear distinctive language of the spirit began to flow from my mouth. That was it! I was baptized in the spirit with the evidence of speaking in tongues.

But I need to balance this testimony so that nobody thinks that the Holy Spirit will come upon you after a prolonged period of waiting. You can pray now, and the Holy Spirit fills you instantly. I have seen that kind of result different times when I pray for people over the phone some won't even take up to 20 minutes before the spirit of God fills his people.

They key thing here is the consistency of asking. Don't just give up because you didn't get filled at the time you prayed. During the time that I was waiting for the Lord to fill me with the Holy Spirit, my hunger and passion to be baptized in tongues never ceased. In fact, day by day it grew. And since my expectation was still high, the Lord had to fulfill his promises in my life (Proverbs 18:23). For anyone who will not cease and stand in faith, without easily giving up God will make sure that the Holy Ghost experience becomes his lot.

The Bible encourages us not to quit like men. But we are told to stand firm until God brings to pass his promises. Whether you are praying for yourself or praying for another person to be filled with the Holy Spirit so that the person can begin to pray in tongues, stand until God fulfills his word.

Prayer to wait and be firm

Father in the mighty name of Jesus, I trust in the power of your promises to fill me right now are or to fill brother (mention brother's name or sister's name if you are praying for another person to be filled with the Holy Ghost) and I asked for the grace to wait no matter what to receive the baptism of the Holy Ghost upon the life of this person I am praying for. We have been told in your word not to quit like men and to be strong believing that you will do it. Father, at this moment I bring to your remembrance your infallible word that the baptism of the Holy Ghost must happen right now in the name of Jesus, Amen.

The prayer I am about to lead you to do below is for those who have prayed for others or themselves and didn't get baptized immediately.

Baptism of the Holy Ghost Prayer Book

Father in the mighty name of Jesus, I know that your word is true and your promises are yes and Amen. I refused to be discouraged and give up on the third person of the Trinity, the Holy Spirit which you said you will give to everyone that asks of you. I pray that you pour him upon me right now in the name of Jesus so that your word and your promises in my life will be fulfilled, in the name of Jesus.

Lord Jesus, I make demands for the grace to consistently knock on heaven's doors until I am filled with the Holy Spirit evidenced by speaking in tongues. Supply me with the grace not to give up easily as I wait on the promise of the Holy Ghost. You have said that we will receive power after that the Holy Ghost has come upon us and we will be witnesses unto you from Jerusalem to the whole world.

Proverbs 6:27

Can a man take fire in his bosom, and his clothes not be burned?

CHAPTER 7

Prayers after Baptism

Praise God because you have now been baptized in the Holy Ghost with the evidence of speaking in tongues. A new personality made an entrance into your life. And he gladly announced his appearance in your life by filling you with the Holy Ghost so that you can speak in tongues. I believe that the Holy Ghost does this on purpose so that no one can say that I didn't even know if he was in my life. But the moment you got baptized with the Holy Ghost and you spoke in tongues, it is a piece of evidence onto you that he is now present in your life.

I know this is a prayer book to guide you on how to be baptized with the Holy Ghost with evidence of speaking in tongues, but I will be doing you a great injustice if I don't prepare you for the life after the baptism of the Holy Ghost. For this purpose, this chapter contains prayers that will help you live the post-Holy Ghost baptism life.

After you have prayed the baptism of the Holy Ghost on the life of a person, you need to guide them. There are several spiritual books written on the post-Holy Ghost baptism life, that is, life after the baptism of the Holy Ghost evidenced by praying tongues. I can recommend so many of these books to you, but you need to be prepared. You have someone who is new in your life, and you need to take time in knowing him. For instance, when two couples get married, they take their time to know one another until they can begin to read hidden codes in facial expression. Whether you prayed for someone to be baptized with the Holy Ghost or you prayed for yourself, you have to prepare yourself to live a life in the spirit.

Prayer for Clarity of His Voice

As a believer, the Holy Ghost is the sole medium by which we hear the voice of God in our day.

John 16:13

> *Howbeit when he, the Spirit of truth, is come, he will guide you into all truth: for he shall not speak of himself; but whatsoever he shall hear, that shall he speak: and he will shew you things to come.*

Now that the Holy Spirit is present in your life, you will be able to hear the voice of God. Every believer who hears God hears his voice through the Holy Spirit.

Without him, it is impossible for God to talk to us. I don't want to go into the details of hearing the voice of God because I have a book that contains all of that. You can check this book on Amazon, How to Hear God's Voice: A believer's Manual to Talking with God.

Hebrews 1:1-2

> *1 God, who at sundry times and in divers manners spake in time past unto the fathers by the prophets,*
>
> *2 Hath in these last days spoken unto us by his Son, whom he hath appointed heir of all things, by whom also he made the worlds;*

The Bible says God speaks to us through his son. And the Son speaks to us through the Holy Ghost.

Prayer

Thank you, father, for pouring your spirit upon me, now I can pray in tongues, the language of the spirit. Let your name be praised for the gift of the spirit in my life. Father, I pray for the ability to hear the Holy Spirit as he talks to me from today in the name of Jesus. I pray for clarity of the voice of the spirit in my ear in the mighty name of Jesus, Amen.

Father in the name of Jesus, I make demands for the grace and the spirit of sensitivity in the name of Jesus. I know that it is not all the time that the Holy Ghost will speak by his voice. I know that sometimes he may drop some things in my heart through impression. I asked you, Lord, to give me the grace to be very sensitive to your spirit as he speaks to me or impresses things upon my heart. I ask all these through faith in your name in the name of Jesus.

Prayer for Obedience

Obedience to the spirit of God is very important. The Holy Spirit is a very gentle spirit of God and that is why he manifests himself through Scriptures in the form of a dove. The dove aspect of the spirit of God is to show us that he is gentle.

Matthew 10:16

> *Behold, I send you forth as sheep in the midst of wolves: be ye therefore wise as serpents, and harmless as doves.*

God wouldn't want to have a wrestling match with you before you obey his instructions. In Scriptures, those who found it a pleasure obeying the voice of God through the Holy Ghost are some of the most blessed people that you can ever find as you read your Bible. God values

Baptism of the Holy Ghost Prayer Book

his spirit and if you are a son or daughter of God, you must also do the same thing. One of the main reasons why the spirit of God left in the book of Genesis chapter 6 versus three was because the people were struggling with the Spirit of God. Whenever disobedience is present, the Holy Spirit withdraws. This has necessitated the inclusion of these post baptism Prayers.

Father in the mighty name of Jesus, I ask for the grace to obey all instructions that the Holy Ghost will be passing to me throughout my life in the name of Jesus. I further ask that none of the instructions that the Holy Spirit gives to me will fall to the ground. I pray for the spirit and the grace of obedience to come upon my life right now in the name of Jesus. I want to be like a tree planted by the rivers of water that will bring forth fruits of obedience in every due season in the name of Jesus.

Father, I know that delayed obedience is no obedience at all. I, therefore, pray for the grace to obey your instruction quickly in the name of Jesus. Help me to be fervent in the way I obey instructions without delay in the name of Jesus.

Father in the mighty name of Jesus, I asked for the grace to obey the instructions the way they were given unto me in the name of Jesus. I ask that you help me to obey the instructions in just the way you give them in Jesus name. Help me not to obey your instruction according to the desires of my heart, but according to your perfect will in the name of Jesus.

Grieving the Holy Spirit

If you want the Holy Spirit to continue to be in your life as your friend, comforter, teacher, and instructor, then you must avoid grieving the Holy Spirit.

Genesis 6:3

And the Lord said, My spirit shall not always strive with man, for that he also is flesh: yet his days shall be an hundred and twenty years.

Anything that the Holy Spirit is not happy with don't do it. If you keep on doing what the spirit detests, he will be grieved. And whenever you grieve the Holy Spirit, and you refuse to repent of that sin, the Holy Spirit withdraws his presence in your life. To this effect, there are many tongue speakers who are praying in the language of the spirit without knowing that the Holy Ghost has long left them. One thing to know is that the Holy Spirit comes with an announcement of his presence in your life, but when he wants to leave, he leaves quietly without telling the person that he has left.

Ephesians 4:30

> **And grieve not the holy Spirit of God, whereby ye are sealed unto the day of redemption.**

Judges 16:20

> **And she said, The Philistines be upon thee, Samson. And he awoke out of his sleep, and said, I will go out as at other times before, and shake myself. And he wist not that the Lord was departed from him.**

Samson did not even know that the spirit of God has left him. He was walking in the deep assumption that the Holy Ghost was with him. Until when the Philistines came upon him, and the source of his strength had gone.

If you want to enjoy a life that is full of the spirit of God, avoid doing things that will grieve the spirit. He won't strife with you if you want to keep doing things that displease him. What the Holy Spirit will

Baptism of the Holy Ghost Prayer Book

do is to leave you quietly. The Bible cautions us in the book of Ephesians 4:30 that we should not grieve the Holy Spirit with whom we have been sealed for the day of redemption. The Holy Spirit living inside of you is a mark of God's ownership over your life. All those who belong to Jesus have the spirit of God in them. The Bible says the Holy Spirit is the seal or mark that shows that we are God's. So, on the rapture day, it is only those who have the seal of the mark of God upon their foreheads or upon them – shall be redeemed. If you grieve the Holy Spirit and he departs out of your life, that seal has been broken. I need to tell you this so that you will know why the Holy Spirit leaves some people.

Even Jesus, our master, had to act cautiously in order not to grieve the Holy Spirit. We can see that in the book of John 8:29 Jesus said that the father has not left him alone because he was doing the things that always made the father happy. And the father's presence in the life of Jesus was marked by the evidence of the spirit of God in his life (Acts 10:38).

As mighty as Jesus was when he ministered on earth, he had to depend entirely on the Holy Spirit. And he successfully did that and died. When the time came for his resurrection, he also had to depend on the Holy Spirit to come out of the grave (Romans 8:11). I say this with all humility and honor to God, I believe that without the Holy Spirit, the plan of God for the salvation of man will have almost been impossible.

And one thing I have come to notice in my little walk with God is that, in our present generation, everything has been reduced to the work of the spirit. The Bible says and it will come to pass in those days, that I will write my laws in their hearts. How is God able to write his laws in our hearts? God was able to do that through the Holy Spirit that lives in us. It is a Holy Spirit that reminds you of God's commandment and convicts you when you do what is wrong before the eyes of the Lord. If all that I have said is appealing to you concerning the Holy Spirit, then don't do anything that will grieve him.

Prayer

Father in the name of Jesus I ask for the grace not to grieve your spirit in the name of Jesus. Help me to keep in step with the Holy Spirit in every area of my life in the mighty name of Jesus so that I don't do anything that would displease him.

Father in the name of Jesus I make demands on your help, being the giver of the spirit of God that you supply me with grace and power to make you happy through your spirit in the name of Jesus. Help me oh Lord, in Jesus name, Amen.

Prayer for the Use of Spiritual Gifts

1 Corinthians 12:1, 4-11

Now concerning spiritual gifts, brethren, I would not have you ignorant.

4 Now there are diversities of gifts, but the same Spirit.

5 And there are differences of administrations, but the same Lord.

6 And there are diversities of operations, but it is the same God which worketh all in all.

7 But the manifestation of the Spirit is given to every man to profit withal.

8 For to one is given by the Spirit the word of wisdom; to another the word of knowledge by the same Spirit;

9 To another faith by the same Spirit; to another the gifts of healing by the same Spirit;

Baptism of the Holy Ghost Prayer Book

10 To another the working of miracles; to another prophecy; to another discerning of spirits; to another divers kinds of tongues; to another the interpretation of tongues:

11 But all these worketh that one and the selfsame Spirit, dividing to every man severally as he will.

The Bible says we should earnestly desire the gift of the spirit. And in the book of Acts 1:8 we are told that you shall receive power after that the Holy Ghost has come upon you and you shall be witnesses unto me in Judaea, Samaria, in Jerusalem, and to the uttermost parts of the earth. The fire of the Holy Spirit that you received on that day when you minister to yourself or ministered to another person to be baptized in the Holy Spirit with the evidence of speaking in tongues, is more than just praying in a strange language of the spirit. What came upon you on that day is power so that you can lead the life that God wants you to live. Towards this end, the power of the Holy Spirit that came upon you is wrapped in diversities of the gift.

The baptism of the Holy Ghost is the key that enables your gifting to bless the body of Christ. The gift of the spirit is already deposited in your life; what happens is the day that the Holy Spirit comes upon your life, he activates those gifts that the father has placed upon your life at the time of your creation.

1 Timothy 4:14

> *Neglect not the gift that is in thee, which was given thee by prophecy, with the laying on of the hands of the presbytery.*

The Scripture tells us that the gifts of the spirit can be developed. Although I am not getting into that for now, what I want you to notice from the Scripture quoted above is that the gift of the spirit of God upon the life of a man can be lying dormant. But when the Holy Spirit comes upon the life of a man, he pours his fire upon these gifts. After that, the man begins to use the gift of the spirit upon his life. Many people did not actually know they had certain gifts in their lives until they had an encounter with the Holy Spirit. That was when they realized that they had the gift of healing all this time in their lives.

Prayer

Father in the name of Jesus, I pray for the grace to be able to use the gifts of the spirit in my life for the profit of the body of Christ in the name of Jesus. I pray that through the gift of the spirit upon my life many will turn to Christ in the name of Jesus. Thank you father, in Jesus name, Amen.

Father in the mighty name of Jesus, I ask for the grace to use my gift to serve the body of Christ in the name of Jesus. Through the gift of the spirit in my life, many mighty works will be done to the glory of your name in the name of Jesus. Thank you, father, for answering my prayer, in Jesus name, Amen.

Matthew 3:11

I indeed baptize you with water unto repentance: but he that cometh after me is mightier than I, whose shoes I am not worthy to bear: he shall baptize you with the Holy Ghost, and with fire:

Proverbs 6:27

Can a man take fire in his bosom, and his clothes not be burned?

Thank you, father, for the release of the power of the Holy Ghost in my life. Thank you because a new fire has been set right now in my bosom. To you be all the glory in the name of Jesus. I give you praise because I cannot carry the same fire you used while on earth to heal the sick, cast out devils, set the captives free, destroy the works of darkness, and bring salvation to mankind and remained the same. I thank you because this fire is going to transform me from an ordinary believer to a supernatural child of God. In the name of Jesus, Amen.

Romans 8:26

> **Likewise the Spirit also helpeth our infirmities: for we know not what we should pray for as we ought: but the Spirit itself maketh intercession for us with groanings which cannot be uttered.**

Luke Luke 2:27

> **And he came by the Spirit into the temple: and when the parents brought in the child**

Jesus, to do for him after the custom of the law,

Almighty father, I want to thank you for the special gift you have given unto me today. Today I saw the manifestation of the Scripture that says that I will receive fire after the Holy Spirit has come upon me and that I will be a witness unto you in all of the earth. Today Lord, that Scripture has been made a reality in my own life. I thank you because this fire will help me to pray as I ought to. I ask that the spirit of God will guide me in praying as I should. I pray for the grace to use this privilege of the fire of the Holy Spirit to serve you. I am aware that by your word, prayer is one of the service one can render to God, in Jesus name, Amen.

John 16:13

> *13 Howbeit when he, the Spirit of truth, is come, he will guide you into all truth: for he shall not speak of himself; but whatsoever he shall hear,*

that shall he speak: and he will shew you things to come.

Romans 8:14

For as many as are led by the Spirit of God, they are the sons of God.

Father, I thank you for giving me the privilege to carry the most precious spirit on the face of the earth. I thank you because all those who received your spirit in their lives have been distinguished as the Holy Spirit guided them to fulfill the divine destiny in you. I thank you because I am also in the same category as all these great men and women. I believe from today, that the Holy Spirit will guide me to walk in divine direction in the name of Jesus. I will no longer miss my step in life or walk through trial and error but will rather follow the path of divine direction as the Holy Spirit leads me in the name of Jesus

John 14:26

__But the Comforter, which is the Holy Ghost, whom the Father will send in my name, he shall teach you all things, and bring all things to your remembrance, whatsoever I have said unto you.__

Father, I thank you for giving me the greatest teacher that the world has ever known. I give you all the praise and glory for the Holy Ghost will teach me all that I need to know in life in Jesus name. I pray for the grace to receive his teaching with meekness and humility so that I will be able to fulfill my destiny in you in the name of Jesus. Thank you, father, for this wonderful teacher which you have graciously given to me in the mighty name of Jesus. Amen.

John 7:38

*He that believeth on me,
as the scripture hath said,
out of his belly shall flow
rivers of living water.*

CHAPTER 8

Your Faith and Baptism

It has been emphasized that the baptism of the Holy Ghost unlocks the vault of gift that God has placed inside of you when you were created or formed. I am a firm believer in the fact that no man is ever empty. Every man you see has something that God has placed inside of him. That is why it is called the body of Christ. The human body comprises of different organs. As little as the eye may look, without it functioning effectively, the

Baptism of the Holy Ghost Prayer Book

entire body cannot go anywhere. It will remain in perpetual darkness without knowing where to go to. I may not know, but I believe that God's intention is for us to work together. The man who is the eyes will need the ear to function well. Another person who is the legs will need the eyes to be able to see what lies ahead of him. It is a body. I have never seen where single eyes made up a human body.

This accounts for the reason why no man is ever empty. God has given to every man according to the measure of grace expressed in the gift of the Holy Spirit.

On the day of your baptism in the Holy Spirit with the evidence of praying in tongues, it is the initial deposit of God upon your life that the Holy Spirit breathes upon. Remember when Jesus was about to leave the earth, he breathed upon the disciples and said, receive you the Holy Ghost. It is this breadth of the Holy Spirit that activates your gifts. It is important to draw this line of explanation so that nobody believes that the moment the Holy Spirit comes upon his life, he will be able to operate in all the gift of the spirit of God. Other gifts of the spirit of God will come upon you as you faithfully walk before him in obedience and service.

If what God has given you is the gift of healing, then the Holy Spirit will activate that gift so that it can be used to serve the body of Christ and to save the lost (Matthew 25:14-30). This does not mean that the gift of the spirit of God will not find expression in your life. Of course, they will manifest. But your strength will lie in your major gift which is the gift of healing.

1 Corinthians 14:1

> *Follow after charity, and desire spiritual gifts, but rather that ye may prophesy.*

1 Corinthians 13:13

13 And now abideth faith, hope, charity, these three; but the greatest of these is charity.

If there are other gifts of the spirit which you desire, you may need to consciously pray those gifts into your life. The Bible tells us to earnestly desire the gift of the spirit. This requires a very conscious effort in order to bring those gifts into manifestation in your life. If you ask, you will surely receive (Matthew 7:7).

The other gifts of the spirit can be received into your life by faith. You make demands for the gift of the spirit of God through prayer. Every gift of God that you see upon the life of any believer on earth, can be contacted and transferred to you. Besides praying to receive the gift of the Holy Spirit, one way to receive the gift of the Holy Spirit is through impartation from brethren who already have that same gift. You can pray for them so that the gift of God upon their lives can rob on you. You can even sow a seed into their lives. Service can also be used to obtain the gift of the Holy Spirit from the life of another believer.

Prayer

Lord, I want to thank you for the baptism of the Holy Spirit that has made it possible for me to walk in my original gift of the spirit of God. I thank you mighty father because this is not the only gift of the spirit that I will walk in.

Father in the mighty name of Jesus, I pray for the activation of other gifts of the spirit in my life in Jesus name. I pray that all the gift of the spirit which are not present in my life be activated in the name of Jesus. I ask that this other gift of the spirit of God will begin to work. In the name of Jesus, Amen.

The Rivers of Living Water

John 7:38

He that believeth on me, as the scripture hath said, out of his belly shall flow rivers of living water.

Jesus was speaking at a feast, and he was telling the people that all of them that believe in him out of their stomach shall flow rivers of living water. I believe that the giver of the fountain of that living water is the Holy Ghost. For you to be an effective believer on earth, the Holy Spirit must be abiding in you. Now, God's intention is not for you to receive the living water and be rejoicing that you have it. God's intendment is so that the living water can touch the lives of people around you. That is the essence of Christianity. When a man is saved and receive the baptism of the Holy Spirit, he should be able to change the world around him.

Prayer

Father in the name of Jesus, I am making demands for your help so that the living water that is in my belly through the baptism of the Holy Spirit will be felt by the people around me in the name of Jesus. Through that same water, I pray for the grace to impart and change my world in the name of Jesus Amen.

Thank you, Lord, for this great gift of the spirit. Now that the living water is flowing from my belly, I pray for the grace to lead a life that will transform people around me in Jesus name. It was the same spirit that was upon the life of Jesus which you used to give salvation to mankind. Hallelujah to your name, that same Holy Ghost is now upon my life. And from my belly, fountains of living water will continue to flow to impart my generation in the name of Jesus. Amen. Thank you mighty father for this deposit of the spirit of God in my life. I know from today that this fountain of living water

Baptism of the Holy Ghost Prayer Book

will begin to speak by touching people around me in the mighty name of Jesus, Amen.

Pius Joseph

Free E-book For You!!!

Download this e-book for free and receive our spiritual enhancing contents

Baptism of the Holy Ghost Prayer Book

https://bit.ly/2W4qgLK

Other books by the same Author

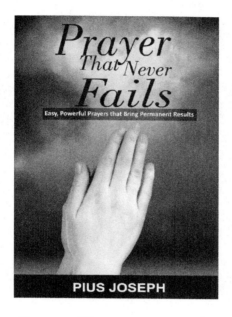

Prayer That Never Fails

Pius Joseph

VISION
FROM THE
HEAVENLY

PIUS
JOSEPH

Baptism of the Holy Ghost Prayer Book

Vision From The Heavenly - Kindle edition by Pius Joseph. Religion & Spirituality Kindle eBook

Check our blog: www.thetentofglory.com

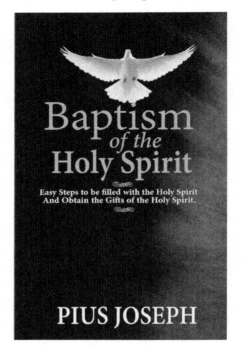

BAPTISM OF THE HOLY SPIRIT: Easy Steps to be Filled With the Holy Spirit And Obtain the Gifts of the Holy Spirit - Kindle edition by Pius Joseph. Religion & Spirituality Kindle eBooks @ Amazon.com.

Printed in Great Britain
by Amazon